HIPPOPOTAMUS

AFRICAN ANIMAL DISCOVERY LIBRARY

Lynn M. Stone

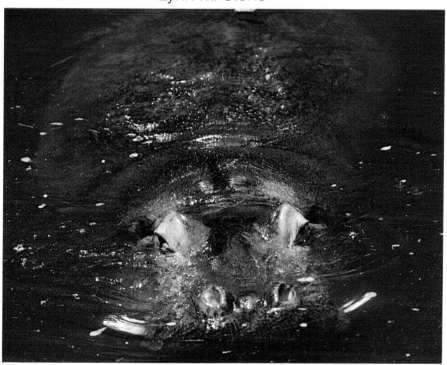

Rourke Corporation, Inc.
Vero Beach, Florida 32964

PHOTO CREDITS

All photos by the Author

LIBRARY OF CONGRESS
Library of Congress Cataloging-in-Publication Data
Stone, Lynn M.
  Hippopotamus / by Lynn M. Stone.

    p. cm. — (African animal discovery library)
    Summary: Describes the physical characteristics, habitat, and
  behavior of the hippopotamus.
    ISBN 0-86593-051-1
    1. Hippopotamus—Juvenile literature. [1. Hippopotamus.]
  I. Title. II. Series: Stone, Lynn M. African animal discovery
  library.
  QL737.U57S76   1990
  599.73'4—dc20   89-48444
                                      CIP
  Printed in the USA   AC

Hippopotamus swimming

TABLE OF CONTENTS

THE HIPPOPOTAMUS

African rivers do not make very safe swimming holes. In addition to crocodiles, they are home for one of the largest animals on earth, the hippopotamus *(Hippopotamus amphibius).*

Hippos don't eat people. Hippos are plant eaters, but they weigh up to 10,000 pounds, and they are not very good-natured. People who know the hippo avoid getting too close.

The only land animals that outweigh a big hippo are the African and Indian elephants.

Hippos spend some time on land. They are most at home, however, in the water.

Hippopotamus

THE HIPPO'S COUSINS

The hippo belongs to a large group of mammals. It includes camels, pigs, antelopes, and many other animals with an even number of toes on each foot.

Elephants and rhinos are large, gray mammals like hippos, but neither is a close cousin of the hippo.

The hippo's closest cousin is the pygmy hippopotamus *(Choeropsis liberiensis).* The pygmy hippo lives only in the wet, rainy forests of West Africa.

The pygmy hippo weighs just 350 to 600 pounds. It spends much more time on land than the common hippo.

Pygmy hippopotamus

HOW THEY LOOK

Hippos aren't well dressed. Like all mammals, they have hair. But they have only a few long, stiff hairs called **bristles.**

A few bristles grow on the hippo's broad face and on the tip of its tail.

A hippo's mouth is extremely wide and deep. When it's open, the hippo shows off a mouthful of long teeth. One tooth from a hippo's lower jaw may weigh over six pounds.

A hippo's legs aren't much longer than its teeth. The hippo's round belly almost scrapes the ground.

Hippopotamus showing tusks

WHERE THEY LIVE

Africa is a huge mass of land called a **continent.** Wild hippos live only in Africa.

North Africa and the Sahara Desert are too dry for hippos. Hippos live in many wet places south of the Sahara.

The hippo's favorite home, or **habitat,** is a winding river with deep pools. It likes to have grassy or swampy areas nearby.

Hippos are strong swimmers. They often dive for five minutes at a time and walk on river bottoms.

Hippos in Mara River

Hippos in Mara River

HOW THEY LIVE

Hippos spend most of the day in or near water. In the evening they go onto land to feed. They may walk two miles from a river as they look for food.

The skin of a hippo has to go from wet to dry. To keep its skin in good condition, the hippo sweats a reddish oil. People once believed that the hippo sweated blood.

Hippos usually live in groups. Old bull hippos keep younger males away from their groups or **herds** of females and their calves. Bulls fight for control of females. Using their teeth as weapons, they can give each other bloody wounds.

Hippos are noisy. They snort, woof, bellow, and blow water mist through their nostrils.

Hippo pool

THE HIPPO'S BABIES

A mother hippo usually has one baby. A newborn hippo calf weighs from 75 to 125 pounds. A year later, it may weigh 550 pounds.

Hippos grow for several years. A male hippo, for instance, is usually not big enough to fight another bull until it is eight years old.

Hippos in the wild have been known to live over 40 years. Captive hippos have lived for more than 50 years.

Hippos on river bank

PREDATOR AND PREY

A hippo puts its big mouth to good use. A hippo may eat 130 pounds of plants in one meal. No wonder the hippo is barrel-shaped!

Sometimes Africa has a long period when no rain falls. This time of dry weather is called a **drought.** The hippo's food plants die in large numbers, but a hippo can live for weeks without eating if it must.

Full-grown hippos feeding on land keep watch for lions. Otherwise, there are unlikely to be any hunting animals, known as **predators,** that can hurt them.

Baby hippos are sometimes **prey,** or food, for hungry crocodiles.

Hippo on river bluff

HIPPOS AND PEOPLE

Hippos can be a threat to people. A hippo is especially a danger if someone is between the hippo and water. A hippo finds safety in water.

But people have done far more harm to hippos than they have done to people. Hippos have been hunted for their tasty meat, fat, thick skin, and **ivory.**

Hippo teeth, or **tusks,** are made of the rock-hard, white material called ivory. Ivory is very valuable for jewelry.

Hippos have been killed, too, for eating farm crops.

Charging hippo

THE HIPPO'S FUTURE

Hippos have disappeared from much of their **range.**
An animal's range is the area in which it is found. In
South and West Africa, hippos have become rare.

In those parts of East Africa where they are protected,
hippos are common. In a few places, their long, round
bodies line the river banks like huge sausages.

The number of people in Africa is growing quickly.
As people take more land for their homes and crops,
wildlife homes vanish. Hippos will have fewer river
banks and marshy places to call home in the future.

Glossary

bristle (BRISS el)—stiff hair

continent (KON tin ent)—a huge mass of land; one of six such land masses on earth

drought (DROWT)—a long period without rainfall

habitat (HAB a tat)—the kind of place an animal lives in, such as a river

herd (HERD)—a group of large, hoofed animals, such as hippos

ivory (I veree)—hard, whitish material that makes up extra-long teeth in certain mammals such as hippos and elephants

predator (PRED a tor)—an animal that kills other animals for food

prey (PREY)—an animal that is hunted by another for food

range (RAYNGE)—the entire area in which a certain type of animal lives

tusk (TUHSK)—an exceptionally long tooth especially in the hippopotamus, elephant, and walrus

INDEX